Animal
Attraction

Inside the Beastly Singles Scene

Hylas Publishing®
129 Main Street, Ste. C
Irvington, NY 10533
www.hylaspublishing.com

Hylas Publishing
Publisher: Sean Moore
Art Director: Gus Yoo
Editorial Director: Ward Calhoun
Photo Editor: Ben DeWalt

ISBN-13: 978-1-4351-1021-2

Printed and bound in China

First American Edition published in 2008
2 4 6 8 10 9 7 5 3 1

Animal
Attraction

Inside the Beastly Singles Scene

WARD CALHOUN

"That's why the lady is a tramp."

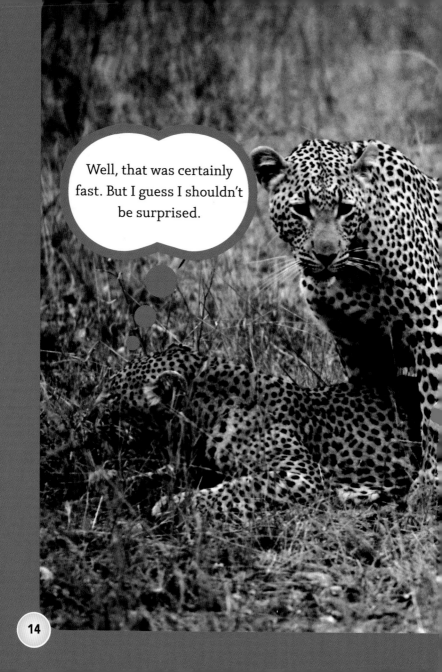

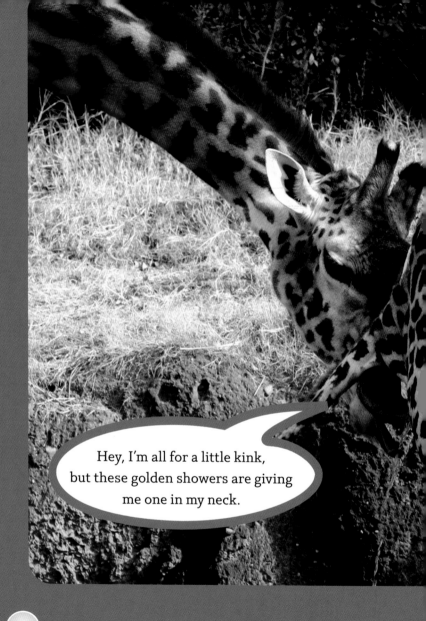

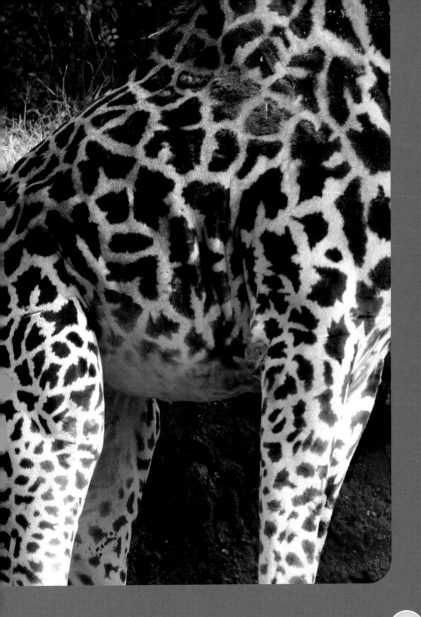

Another kiss on the cheek? Jeez, how many checks does a guy have to pick up?

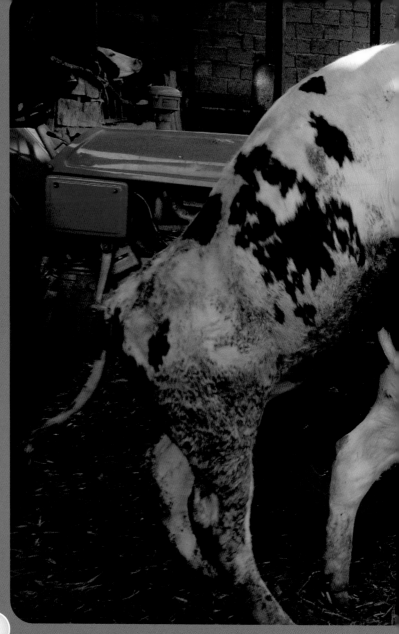

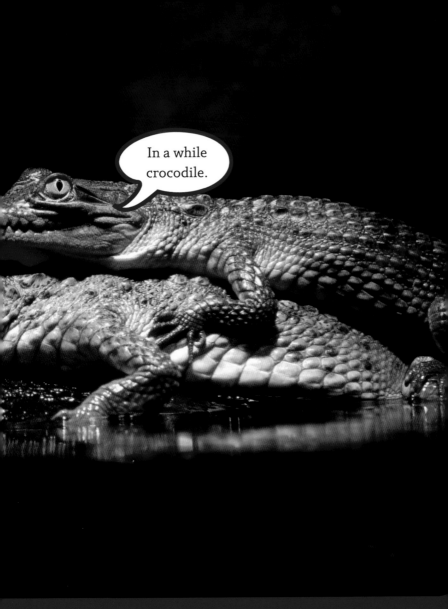

Sheesh! I specifically told the dating service not to set me up with any more dogs.

Sigh— another shrimp on the Barbie.

No, really, when it's not cold it's *this* big!

Well, I guess you just answered the "which came first?" question.

For the last time, *yes* I took the trash out. Now will you please get off my back already?

This is more like a 67, not a 69.

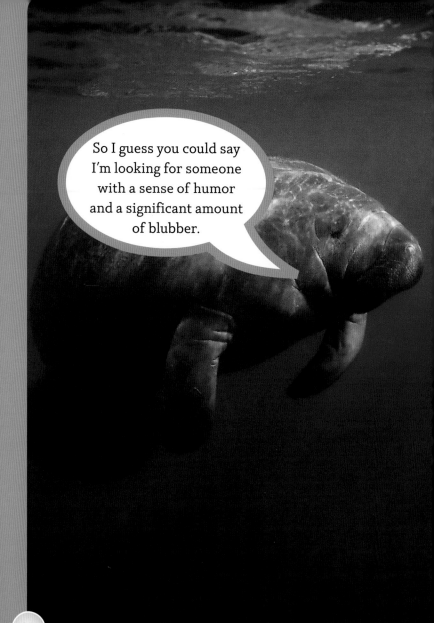

Baby got back.

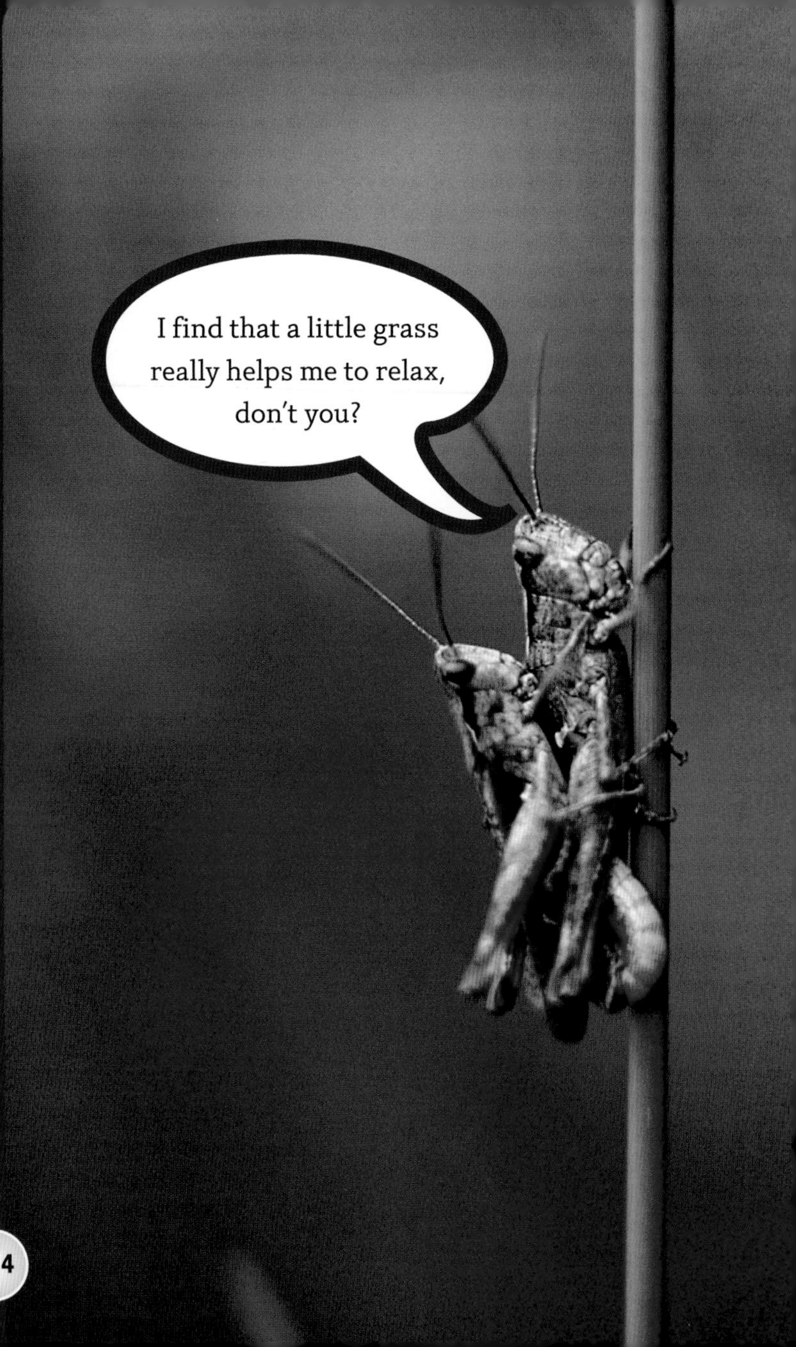
I find that a little grass really helps me to relax, don't you?

Photography Credits

Acknowledgments

The author would like to thank his wife Kimberly for being kind to dumb animals such as himself. This project also benefited greatly from the work of design dynamo Gus Yoo and editorial whiz kid Rachael Lanicci. Finally, special thanks to Ben DeWalt and Matthew Gross for their caption contributions.